Heredity

by Michelle Hyde Parsons

Table of Contents

Introduction 2

Chapter 1 What Is Heredity? 4

Chapter 2 What Are
Chromosomes and Genes? 12

Chapter 3 What Are Some Special Traits? . . . 16

Summary 20

Glossary 22

Index 24

Introduction

Why do people look like they do? Read about **heredity** to find out.

Words to Know

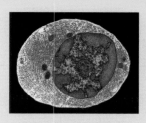 cells

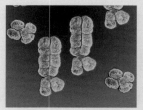 chromosomes

 DNA

 genes

 heredity

 trait

See the Glossary on page 22.

What Is Heredity?

Are your eyes brown? Are your eyes blue?
Are your eyes green?

▲ Your eye color is part of heredity.

The color of your eyes is a **trait**. A trait is part of heredity.

Solve This

Make a chart like this chart. Put information in the chart. Which color has the highest number?

Eye Colors in My Class	
Color	**How Many Students?**
Blue	
Brown	
Green	

Is your hair brown? Is your hair black?
Is your hair blond? Is your hair red?

Your hair color is part of heredity. ▲

The color of your hair is a trait. A trait is part of heredity.

The shape of your body is a trait. A trait is part of heredity.

▲ **Your body shape is part of heredity.**

The shape of your nose is a trait. The shape of your face is a trait. A trait is part of heredity.

▲ Your nose and face shape are part of heredity.

You got your traits from your parents. You inherited your traits from your parents.

▲ This boy inherited traits from his parents.

Often people inherit other traits from parents. What color hair do you have? What color eyes do you have? What body shape do you have?

△ Our traits make us look different from others.

Did You Know?

We can inherit talents from our parents. Can you sing well? Can you draw well? Maybe you inherited these talents from your parents.

What Are Chromosomes and Genes?

Your whole body is **cells**. Your body has millions of cells. Your cells have **chromosomes**.

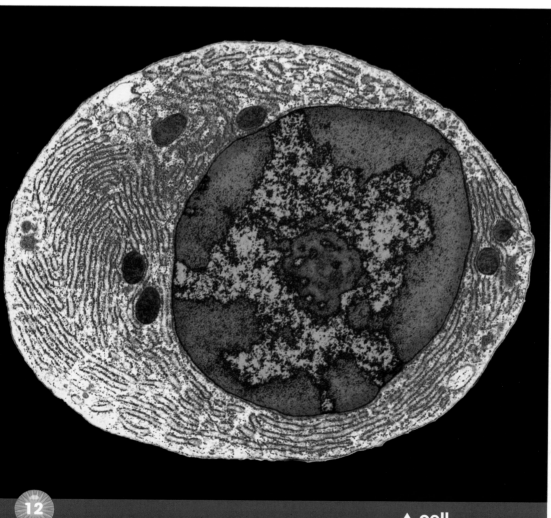

▲ cell

Each cell has 46 chromosomes. Each cell has 23 chromosomes from your mother. Each cell has 23 chromosomes from your father.

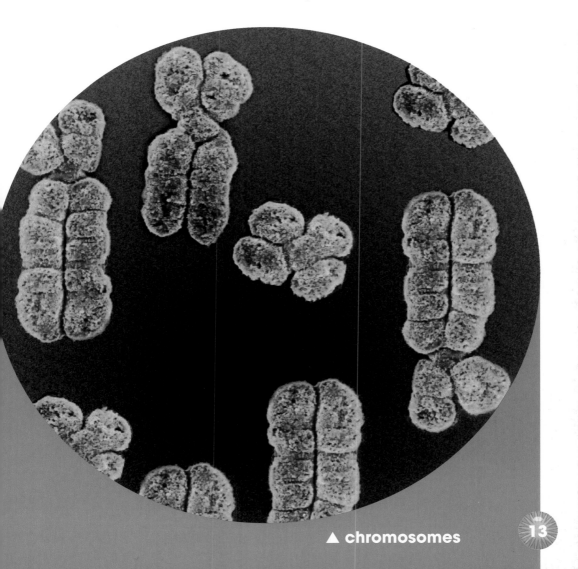

▲ chromosomes

Chromosomes have **DNA**. DNA has **genes**.

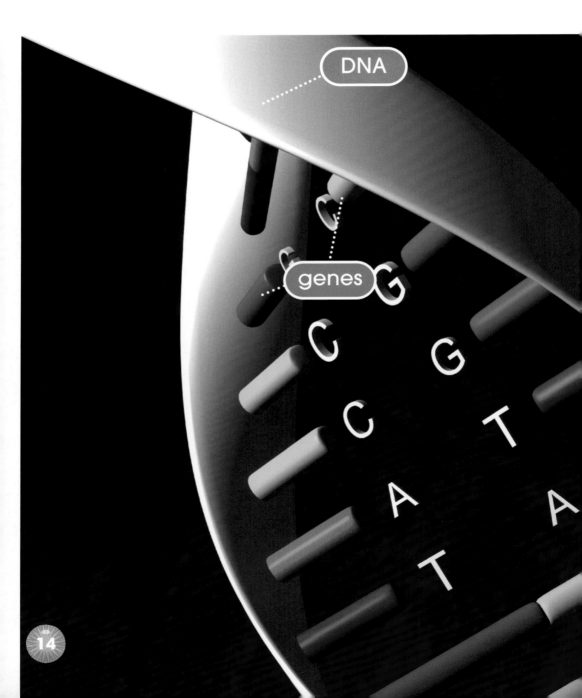

Genes decide what traits you get from your parents. Genes decide what traits you inherit from your parents.

▲ You inherit traits from your parents.

What Are Some Special Traits?

Curling your tongue is a special trait. Can you curl your tongue? Maybe you inherited this trait from your parents.

▲ Curling your tongue is a trait.

Writing with your left hand is a special trait. Do you write with your left hand? Maybe you inherited this trait from your parents.

Having long eyelashes is a special trait. Do you have long eyelashes? Maybe you inherited this trait from your parents.

eyelashes

It's A Fact

Some people cannot see all of the colors. We say these people are color blind. Being color blind is a trait.

Having freckles is a special trait. Do you have freckles? You inherited this trait from your parents.

▲ Having freckles is a trait.

Try This

Wiggling your ears is a special trait. Can you wiggle your ears? Ask your mother to wiggle her ears. Ask your father to wiggle his ears.

19

Summary

You inherited traits from your parents. Traits are part of heredity. Genes decide what traits you inherit. You have special traits, too.

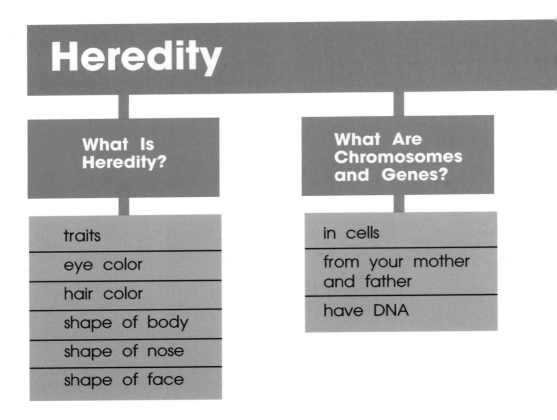

Heredity

What Is Heredity?

traits

eye color

hair color

shape of body

shape of nose

shape of face

What Are Chromosomes and Genes?

in cells

from your mother and father

have DNA

What Are Some Special Traits?

curling your tongue

writing with left hand

long eyelashes

freckles

Think About It

1. What is heredity?
2. How are chromosomes and genes alike?
3. How are chromosomes and genes different?

Glossary

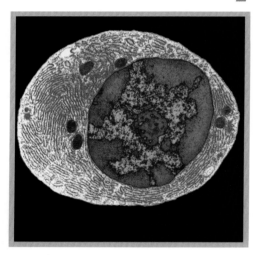

cells the small units that make up your body

Your whole body is made of cells.

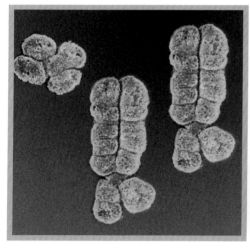

chromosomes parts of cells

Each cell has 46 chromosomes.

DNA part of a chromosome that has genes

DNA is in cells.

genes parts of chromosomes that are in DNA

Genes decide what traits you get from your parents.

heredity traits you get from your parents

*Eye color is part of your **heredity**.*

trait something about your body or a talent

*Hair color is a **trait**.*

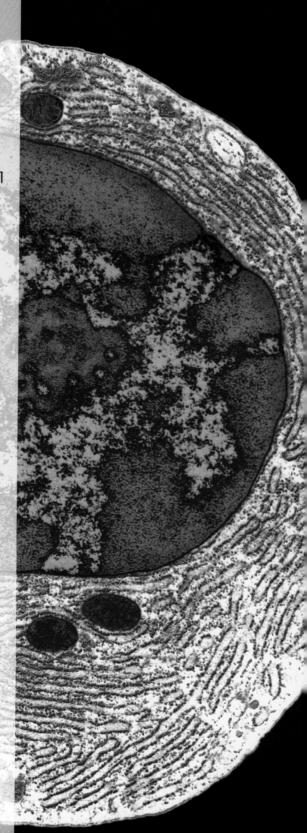

Index

cells, 12, 20

chromosomes, 12–14, 20–21

DNA, 14, 20

ears, 19

eyes, 4–5, 11, 20

genes, 14–15, 20–21

hair, 6–7, 11, 20

heredity, 2, 4–9, 20–21

parents, 10–11, 15–19

tongue, 16, 21

trait, 5, 7–11, 15–20